AWESOME JOKES

FOR 6 YEAR OLDS

SILLY JOKES FOR KIDS AGED 6

What candy is the best in school?

a. Smarties!

Knock knock.
a. Who's there?
b. Harry.
c. Harry who?
d. Harry and open up, it's freezing out here!

Knock knock?
a. Who's there?
b. Interrupting cow.
c. Interrupting c-
d. MOOOOOOOOOOO.

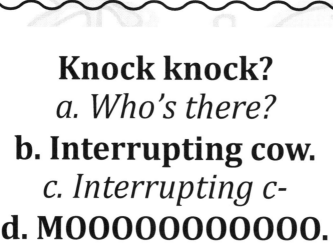

What jiggles and is deadly?

a. Shark infested jello.

Knock knock.

a. Who's there?

b. Leaf.

c. Leaf who?

d. Leaf this house at once!

Why did the chicken cross the park?

a. To get to the other slide.

What does a robotic toad say?

a. Rib-bot.

What kind of car do insects drive?

a. VW Beetles.

How many tickles does it take until an octopus laughs?

a. Ten tickles.

What does a boxer drink on vacation?

a. Hawaiian punch.

What does a witch's vehicle say?

a. BROOOOOOOOM.

What do you find at a cleaner's wedding?

a. A bride and broom!

Where do you buy things to hang up?

a. At Wall-Mart.

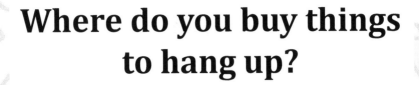

Why did the king's men not like the daytime?

a. Because they were knights.

What do you do when you need to buy new curtains?

a. Go window shopping.

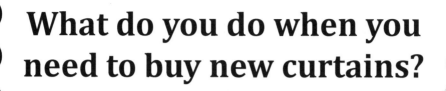

What is the best phone for your vision?

a. The Eye Phone.

What do you call a princess with a big dresser?

a. Snow White and the Seven Drawers.

What is slippery and two feet long?

a. A pair of slippers.

What do you call a big ant?

a. A giAnt.

How did the T-rex feel after going to the gym?

a. Dino "sore."

How do you tell a door that it's cute?

a. Tell it that it's a-door-able.

What do you call a woman who loves hamburgers?

a. Patty.

Why was the cook under arrest?

a. Because she whipped cream and beat eggs.

Why did the fish stay home from work?

a. Because he was feeling eel.

Why are fish so smart?

a. Because they go to school.

What do you call someone who can't stop fishing?

a. Hooked.

What do you call a server at a restaurant who tells you how heavy you are?

a. A weighter.

What is the loudest color?

a. Yell-ow.

Why is Washington D.C. the best place to buy hats?

a. Because it's the cap-ital.

What kind of stories do giraffes like best?

a. Tall tales.

How do you prepare a party that's in outer space?

a. You have to planet.

Why did the man take his toolbox to the salon?

a. Because he wanted to get his nails done.

Why did the man buy his girlfriend a canoe on Valentine's Day?

a. Because he heard a rows was romantic.

What does a phone eat before an entrée?

a. Apps.

Knock knock.
a. Who's there?
b. Little old lady.
c. Little old lady who?
d. Wow, I had no idea you were a yodeler!

How do you get a lumberjack to go on a date with you?

a. You axe him out.

What do you call a man with a lot of money?

a. Rich.

What are the most boring summer shoes?

a. San-dulls.

What do you call it when a bird breaks the law?

a. Ill-eagle.

How did the hunter catch the squirrel?

a. He climbed a tree and acted like a nut.

What is the most mathematical part of the kitchen?

a. The counter.

Why does racing a truck make you sleepy?

a. Because if you run in front you get tired, and if you run behind you get exhausted.

What do you call it when all your faucets run at the same time?

a. In sink.

What did the man on the diet say when he walked into the pastry shop?

a. Donut tempt me.

What do you call a man who likes to give speeches?

a. Mike.

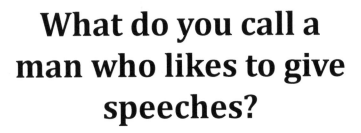

What do you call a carousel made up of cows?

a. A dairy-go-round.

Why did the criminal take a bath before robbing the bank?

a. Because she wanted to make a clean getaway.

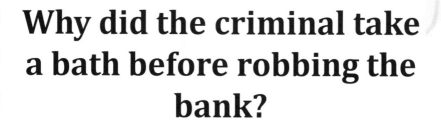

A man walks into a library and says, "Could I have a hamburger please?" The librarian says, "Sir, this is a library."

a. "Oh," says the man, then whispers, "Could I have a hamburger please?"

What kind of flower do you have on your face?

a. Two lips.

What kind of fruit do you always have two of?

a. A pear.

Where did the general keep his armies?

a. In his sleevies.

Why are cows good at the piano?

a. Because they're moo-sical.

Did you hear that my haircutter isn't cutting hair any longer?

a. They're cutting it shorter!

Who can jump higher than a house?

a. Anyone. Houses can't jump.

What thing has a bottom that's at the top?

a. A leg.

What do you call a badger with good behavior?

a. A goodger.

What is a skeleton's favorite store?

a. The body shop.

What is the best time to visit the dentist?

a. At tooth-hurty.

What happened to the chicken who behaved poorly at school?

a. She got eggspelled.

A horse walks into a bar.

a. The bartender asks it, "Why the long face?"

What do you do if your mom turns into a deck of cards?

a. Deal with it.

What do you get if you cross a kangaroo and an elephant?

a. A bunch of holes all across Australia.

What is a frog's favorite soda?

a. Croak-a-Cola.

What is the most popular soda in Australia?

a. Coca-Koala.

What do you call a large animal that doesn't matter?

a. Irrelephant.

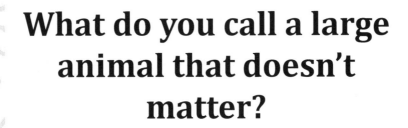

What do you do when a pig gets hurt?

a. Call a hambulance.

How do you know when an elephant is underneath your bed?

a. If your nose is touching the ceiling.

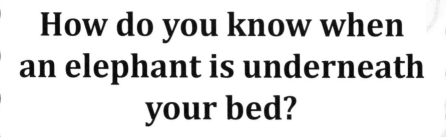

Billy's Mom has four kids. The first three are named April, May, and June. What is the name of the fourth child?

a. Billy.

What does a farmer use in geometry?

a. His pro-tractor.

It smells like updog in here?

a. What's updog?

b. Not much, what's up with you?

When does an astronaut eat dinner?

a. After launch.

What did the snowman say to the other snowman?

a. It smells like carrots.

What do you say when a bird is flying at your head?

a. "Duck!"

Look, a samatta!

a. What's samatta?

b. Nothing, what's samatta with you?

What is orange and smells just like a parrot?

a. A carrot.

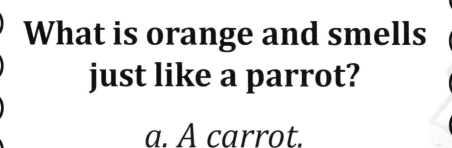

Why did the rabbit nibble on the redhead's hair?

a. Because someone called them a carrot top.

What do you call a cow that lost its legs?

a. Ground beef.

What colors did the artist paint the sun and the wind?

a. The sun rose and the wind blue.

What did the balloon say to the other balloon as they floated through the desert?

a. "Watch out for the cactussssssss."

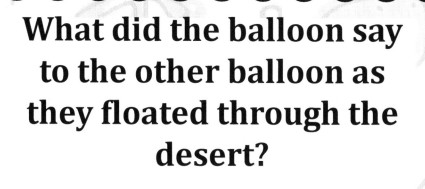

How do you know when an egg finds your joke funny?

a. When it's cracking up.

What do you call it when a piece of bread is doing well?

a. It's on a roll.

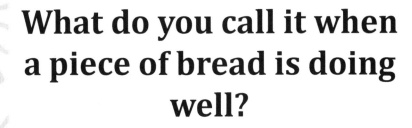

Why do sharks only live in saltwater?

a. Because pepper makes them sneeze.

Why does your nose look puffy?

a. Because I was smelling a brose.

b. There's no B in rose.

c. There was in this one.

Why did the cat get kicked out of the game?

a. Because it was a cheetah.

What did the piece toast wear when it was going to bed?

a. Its pa-jam-as.

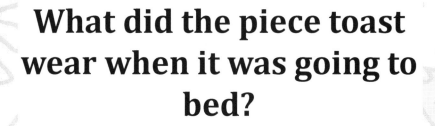

Why was the traveler wearing a cast?

a. Because he went on a trip.

What goes up and down but cannot move at all?

a. Steps.

What did the notebook say to the pen?

a. Write on!

How did Lee feel when no one talked to him?

a. Lonely.

What did the princess say when the copier jammed?

a. Some day my prints will come!

What part of the car always falls asleep?

a. The wheels, because they are always tired.

How long were you in the store?"

a. "About the same length I am now."

What day do you walk in the most?

a. March.

Why is the calendar always going out so much?

a. Because it has so many dates.

Why did Mickey get in the spaceship?

a. Because he wanted to go to Pluto.

My teacher is very careful, but there is one thing she always overlooks.

a. Her nose!

Why did the man throw the clock out the window?

a. Because he wanted to see time fly.

Why did the traffic light spend so much time in the locker room?

a. Because it took so long to change.

Why did the robber shower before he robbed the bank?

a. Because he wanted to have a clean getaway.

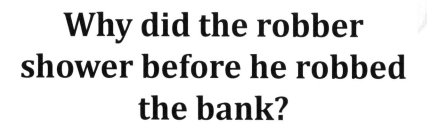

Why did the ketchup thief go to jail?

a. Because he was caught red handed!

Made in United States
Orlando, FL
28 January 2023